Farrago

Bridgett Colwell

Presentation by *BookLeaf Publishing*

Web: www.bookleafpub.com

E-mail: info@bookleafpub.com

ISBN: 9789357614108

First edition 2022

ACKNOWLEDGEMENT

Thank you for everyone who inspired these poems, the good and the bad.
Without you, I wouldn't have felt emotion deep enough to convey in these words.

PREFACE

There is fear and regret,
There is self-loathing and confusion.
There is confidence and joy,
There is love and compassion.
There is a constant war; the victor gets the crown
Chaos reigns supreme.

Dream

I thank the stars tonight that I do not have obligations tomorrow. The sky is crisp in the winter and the dark whisper of night bites through my warmth like biting into an apple. I don't mind it though, it is refreshing. I can hear the wind howl through the walls and shake the windows of this old, bedraggled building. I lay in bed, my head near the window, feeling the chill of the outside whisper through the curtain.

In these moments, I find myself surprised at how easily people are able to put yesterday behind them. I admit, I am envious. To put their head on a pillow and fall into their subconscious like greeting an old friend. I do sleep, but not in sync with common schedules. And never consistently restful. When I can't calm my thoughts, I look outside. I think of the people who have lived, and those who have died. Those I have never met or ones whom I loved from afar. My family, my friends, my lovers and my enemies. I watch days turn to night and spin back into morning, ever fueling my thoughts and anxieties.

I wonder if I'm stretching my time too thinly. It seems as though there is never enough time to do what I want to do. Yet simultaneously, I have too much time. Too much time to ponder and worry and reflect on things I would rather forget. I have more time than most to do these things. While the world dreams, I lay in a waking nightmare, courtesy of my own mind.

It seems, just as I feel my lashes flutter, the sounds of routine and chaos begin to assemble in the streets. The echoes of vehicles grow more frequent, lights flicker on one-by-one, accompanied by the bustling of people as they prepare to go wherever it is they go.

I kiss the last of the dark blue sky adieu and accept the fate of the unrest. Today, I will be plaintive, on edge, and anxious because my mind has not had the necessary recess of sleep. It spent the night racing and has turned on itself. A civil war of self doubt and rational thought rage as I paint on a smile and prepare for 'just another day'.

Equinox

Come with me, my lovely leaves,
Whispers the wind to the trees.
Summer is over, and autumn is here.
Come, alert to the transformation of seasons;
Wearing crimson dresses and coats of gold and
orange.
In the crisp dawn you dance
on your way to the ground;
To cover the roots and wildflowers, shielding
them from winter's frost.
Come lovely leaves,
Whisper the mighty oaks and slender birch,
Nourish your mothers as we once nursed you.
While the bears and bees slumber,
the beetles, birds, and field mice
blanket themselves in the decomposition of your
past life.
You'll generate life in a new dawn,
Once old man Winter
has come and gone.

Desolation

I still smile at pretty things and laugh when
jokes are funny.
I still talk to people and enjoy sunny days.
But when I am alone, I am enveloped in
darkness.
I look in the mirror, and don't like what I see.
I miss things that don't exist.
I am overwhelmed by what was and is and could
be and never will be.
Sometimes, when I'm alone, my world just
crumbles around me.
I'll be perfectly fine and then I won't be.
Just like that.
That quickly, I become engulfed in a raging
storm inside my mind.
I forget what it feels like to smile, to laugh.
All I know is that I'm not okay.
I'm not okay at all.
And the pain in my head becomes pain in my
body.
My muscles ache and my limbs feel weak and
heavy.
My mind is spinning a thousand thoughts a
minute
But mostly I feel...emptiness.

My struggles are my own, not the concern or care of others.
Why burden anyone with pointless shit that I can't even make sense of for myself?
So I just lay here,
Alone.
I cry and my tears feel like acid, burning down my cheeks and chin.
My words keep bleeding out, at such a rapid rate that I can't stop them. I wait for you to stitch me up, silence me, make me feel better.
As if my body is a coffin and I am buried alive.

Falling

The first time she fell, she was just a girl.
The fall was not too far, the land not too hard.
It hurt though; worse than anything she could
remember ever hurting.
She wasn't aware of how painful the falls to
come would be.
As she grew, she kept falling.
Every time scarring her just a little more,
Every time picking herself back up.
Occasionally, someone else would help her up-
Reach down and gently take her hand,
comforting her for just that moment.
But she always fell again, harder; fervid.
One day she fell and couldn't get up.
She lay on the ground, soundless sobs wracking
through her
As tears streamed down her cheeks.
The pain was unbearable, sempiternal.
She didn't move for days.
But eventually, she pulled herself up. She wiped
her face, dusted herself off,
And went on as best as she could, promising
herself she'd never fall again.
She would be very careful, even if it meant
wrapping herself in cushioned protection.

Time went by without incident. She began to feel safe.
She removed the cushions, let herself be free again.
She knew better, she should have stayed guarded.
But she soon felt the familiarity of the fall.
Suddenly, absolutely.
She couldn't help but think to herself, maybe this time will be different.
Maybe this time won't hurt
Maybe, just maybe this time,
He would catch her.

Butterflies and Coffee

Butterflies and coffee
Turned to long walks and drawn out talks
To bad movies, to music, to big-belly laughs
To the books we read together, to our pasts.
To your small room, to my big bed.
To the light in the window, the light in your
eyes, the light in your hair, to all that we've said.
To coffee at midnight, to dinner at dawn.
To kissing so hard our lips were raw with love,
To the unexpected time when two became one.
To our bodies, spilling together, clutched tightly
asleep.
Your leg, my arm, tender touches so deep.
To your smile, to my tears
To our love, to our fears.
To all you had to offer, to everything I had left.
You gave me hope again, that true love did exist.
To short days, to long nights
To arguments but never fights.
To a future, to a home
To never again feeling alone.
To adventures and to staying in,
To being so in love, it makes my head spin.
To butterflies for always, to coffee whenever.
To life, to love, to us forever.

Selcouth

For my entire life, I have thought that all I ever wanted was mountains and seas,
Magnificent city lights, treks through the rain forests, castles and cathedrals.
I never thought one person could satisfy my thirst for adventure.
I never thought that I could be happy in just one place.
But the truth is, I don't care where I am.
I don't care what I'm doing.
As long as I have you.
You are all I ever hoped that love could be.
You are the poem I could never write, the story I always wanted to tell.
I don't want a fairy tale ending with you because I don't want it to end.
I want to be there for your failures as you overcome them.
I want to help you face your fears. When you are shattered and broken, I want to pick up the pieces
and hold you so tightly that you grow back together.
I want to give you the kind of love that is not fake or fabricated,

But real, honest, and raw.
Falling in love with you wasn't ever falling at
all. It was like stepping into a house and
realizing that I was finally home.
And while coffee is amazing, I would rather
have you kiss me awake every morning.
Because, I swear, that every time we kiss, I taste
the next sixty years of my life.
And on my bad days, when the clouds roll over
me and shadow me in darkness,
I hope you kiss me in the rain instead of
fumbling for an umbrella.

Haven

I am not the first person you have loved.
You are not the first mouth I've tasted forever in.
We have both felt the blades of loss and betrayal
cut through our flesh,
searing scars into our hearts.
It is not the future I am afraid of; it is the
repetition of the past.
Things I do not ever want to relive.
But the miracle of you came unannounced.
Like a ship in the night, bombarding the harbor
in a battle of kisses and cuddles.
When I'd given up on love; that is when you
appeared.
And this is how we heal…together.
I will kiss you like forgiveness; you will hold me
like I'm hope.
I will write poems about the scar on your chin,
novels on the smell of salt in your sweat.
I will create new words because the dictionary
does not have what I need to describe the way it
feels to be with you.
And I will not be afraid of your scars.
Because my body houses scars and loves them
into wildflowers.

Every flower we press into the books that we
read will be a promise to each other.
There will be days when you will shine brighter
than all the stars in the sky,
more brilliantly than the sun.
And there will be nights you collapse in my lap,
a broken puddle of grief and uncertainty.
But you will still be the most beautiful thing I
know.

Calamitous Love

Ephemeral nights follow rantipole fights.
Intimacy builds up and we think we may make
it; it could be different this time.
Until that love turns caustic and comes barreling
down in heart stopping waves of hurt.
Until neither of us belong to anything but
beloved memories.
When you no longer feel like home, what are we
fighting for?
What am I defending if "us" is an arduous uphill
battle to an imaginary place that feels like
warmth and comfort?
This calamitous love, this internecine war.
The constant struggle of limerence and
sanguinity and melancholy that leaves us
shell-shocked and wounded.
What is the right side of war?
Do we take up arms and continue fighting or do
we surrender,
raising the white flag to meet permanent
detachment and despondency.
There will be happiness after you.
But there was so much happiness because of
you.
Can this broken mosaic heart be mended again?

Will we be capable of another deep love or will we forever be part of a turbulent battlefield.

Taciturn

I love you. But you don't know how to love.
You can talk about love. You can see love and
feel love and even make love.
But you cannot give love.
And you cannot make promises. I desperately
wanted promises.
I want your heart, but I know I cannot have it.
So I take what I can get.
Temporary bliss.
Passionate highs and lows.
Withdrawal and manipulation, however
unintentional.
You cannot stay still; you have to keep moving.
If you stopped moving, you feel like you will
self-destruct.
If you stop wandering, you will have to face
yourself; your fear, grievances, and sadness.
You choose to stay in the dark where you cannot
see.
You are deathly afraid of your shadow, so you
hide from the sun.
But I love your shadow, I see potential in it.
I thought love could help you, but it pushed you
away.

You knew how much it hurt me but didn't know
how to share anything but pain.
Maybe you are only comfortable in chaos.
I am blinded to what was really happening, only
seeing what I wish would happen.
You value your privacy far more than the
intimacy of sincere connection so you keep your
distance at all costs.
Intimacy could lead to your undoing,
it may be an irrational and indulgent mistake.
Yet I cannot help but feel a sense of privilege for
having such passion in my life.
You stirred something deep inside me, from the
very moment we met.
In a place that I dare not enter, that I cannot stir
myself and that no one else has ever done.
But this is it, a love unrequited.
The infinite curse of the lonely heart.

Alone

It's such a strange misery.
We all feel so alone when it comes, yet everyone
has experienced it.
It's waking up and checking your phone for
messages that aren't there.
It is not being able to watch a show because you
were supposed to finish it together.
It is the sudden awareness of being alone, even
when surrounded by people.
It is the familiarity of them that is missed.
The way you could talk about everything.
No one else wants to hear the details of your day
or see the silly photos you take.
No one else says good morning and goodnight in
a daily routine.
It isn't the goodbye that hurts.
It isn't the period or the ellipsis; it is the spaces
between.
The emptiness, the void.
It is the feeling in the pit of your stomach...like
the butterflies just died.

Compunction

She who comes after me, who you thought
would understand you better, would love you
better,
Would be better…
She will be a prosaic imitation of who I am.
She will write poems on your lips in an attempt
to purge the taste of me.
She will try to kiss her words softly into your
skin in hopes that it will erase my caresses.
She will try to make love to you, but it will be
hard and abrupt, and you will miss my soft
stroking embraces.
She will be a poignant reminder of the woman
you let slip away.
Nothing she does will excite you or intrigue you.
This will break her. YOU will break her as you
did me.
You will break her when she recognizes me in
your eyes.
Me, staring at her with pity… it will hit her,
maybe before it ever even hits you.
How painful it is for her to be in love with a man
who will always be busy loving someone
That he will never get his hands on again.

Innocent

When I was growing up,
I learned that monsters are real.
But they do not live under beds or in eerie
houses or shaded forests.
No, monsters live with us.
They smile at us from across the dinner table,
They pick us up from school,
They buy us shiny trinkets.
These monsters can be charming and look
normal…
Until they corner their prey, ambushing them in
the night.

In a shadowed room of a quiet house,
When the dogs were out walking and the birds
gleefully flitted in the sun,
Is where you kidnapped childhoods.
Your malodorous breath, reeking of cigars and
stale coffee,
Whispered harsh commands
While your calloused hands hungrily sought
pleasure in my adolescent body.
The salacious darkness of your soul forever
stained my honey heart,

Inking it black where it should be bright.
Every abrasive caress is another year of isolation
and calamity.
Every mocking embrace is another relationship
of distrust and sabotage.
Every lecherous game is a loss of self-worth and
disorientation.
Decades later, my colors are still muddied,
My heart still splotchy with shades of black and
red.
Science says that every seven years, bodies
generate new cells, fully and completely.
It's nice to know that by now
my skin, my hair, my lips, my groin,
have never been touched by you.
But my mind doesn't generate new memories.
I cannot will into existence a heroic you.
I cannot even fathom a decent you.
You were not the monster under my bed but in it.
After the events had come and passed,
A little girl grew up too fast.

Nova

They wanted her to be the sun;
Shining vividly, spreading warmth, bringing life
to all around.
But the sun can be painful.
They complained of the heat, they complained
of the burns.
They couldn't look directly at her because her
radiance was blinding.
When she was muted, they complained.
When she was bright, they hid.
As much as they wanted her to be the sun,
they only appreciated her beauty when she was
leaving and missed her when she was gone.
She wanted to be the moon.
Full of wonder and mystery. Always changing.
Still shining brightly but surrounded by millions
of flickering crystals
And while drowning in the darkest of shadows,
She can light the way home.
The Sun and Moon shone independently and
with omnipotence.
Their love for one another was inexorable
though fleeting,
Always yearning and searching for the other
She was the Sun, she was the Moon

She had galaxies in her eyes
And a black hole in her heart.

Chronic

I hate when I have to cancel,
Again and over again
When I'm losing friend after friend
And I wonder if it will end.
I know I don't look sick,
I know you think I'm lazy, and it's all just in my
head.
But every moment that I struggle
To just make it out of bed.
An illness that you cannot see,
Is slowly draining me.
It hurts when you don't believe, or feel empathy,
or care.
It's hard to muster the will to function, to go to
work or use the stairs.
I want to do it all; I want to have a life…
But how can I go on adventures when my
insides are being knifed.
I've lost my ability to mother, to nurture and
adore.
And liking me for who I am, well that is a major
chore.
I am so tired of being sick, so sick of being tired.
I promise I am not unreliable; it is my body that
should be fired.

Those that know and love me,
Must understand my reality.

Spectrum

Oh beautiful one with stars in your eyes,
The wonder of you defines magic.
Your soul holds the secrets of the universe
But you keep those answers sealed behind
closed lips.
You captivate, charm, and entrance the world as
you come at it head-on.
You vibrate on a different frequency, but it is
pure and free.
You are every color of the rainbow; yet do not
know how to display this kaleidoscope.
You enlighten others in patience, compassion,
empathy, mindfulness...
Even when you display quite the opposite.
I feel the joy in your clapping, the pain when
you cry, the frustration from the unexpected...
But I also see your colors radiating vibrantly in
all you do.
When the world tries to anchor you; fly far
away.
Fly free and fly high...just don't lose sight of the
earth.
For you are the most beautiful of creations,
To those on the ground who see the true you.

Sanctuary

We as humans require that things be mysterious
and unexplored.
That the land and sea be untamed and wild,
indefinitely.
Unfathomed by us because they themselves are
unfathomable.
We have a yearning to explore them, to become
one.
We need to be in nature.
The clearest ways to the answers of the universe
and to life are through unpaved forests;
In the whispers of the leaves and the churning of
the tides.
We must adopt the pace of nature, for she is
patient.
We must see that nothing is perfect; but
everything is perfect.
Nature is chaotic and powerful and gorgeous and
gentle and unwavering.
When the mountains echo your name and the
rain hums its' lullabies,
When the smell of the earth awakens your
senses and the oceans' song drums in your ear,
How can you choose a concrete prison,
surrounded by horns and idle chatter?

Embrace the warmth of the sun, the mystery of
the stars, the colors of autumn and the simple
beauty of the wildflower,
For they are calling you home.

Inferno

Once upon a time,
I set fire to the sky in hopes that you would
notice me;
But you just let the whole world burn.
And isn't it frightening, how you can fall in a
love so deep, in just a fraction of a second
That it takes a whole lifetime to get over.
Loving you was my most exquisite form of
self-destruction.
When I was your cure, you were the disease.
While I was saving you, you were killing me.
What I have learned is this:
Romanticizing the past is more dangerous than
sanguinizing the future.
We build mirages out of memories and worship
them like gods.
In these false recollections, you were attentive
and compassionate.
But I had formed you into who I hoped you
could be,
And forgotten who you really were.
You are the one who lit up my life…
In the way that gave me third degree burns on
my heart and left me scarred forever.

Home

The end of the world will not come swiftly,
Not as a plague, pandemic, nor war.
But it arrives slowly, in stages.
Warnings come, but they go ignored.
We choose to push them aside.
"It's not our fault, it's not our problem."
We chew on the fattened overpopulation of
humanity.
We gorge ourselves with fossil fuels and
non-renewable resources.
Yet we cannot satiate our hunger.
Riding the warming waves of climate change...
While lush green coasts become arid and
lifeless,
Glaciers melt and oceans rise,
Mountains become islands.
Mass extinction creeps through and entire
ecosystems are lost...
And as the trees burn and the bees disappear.
Our children's children will listen to stories.
of wildflowers, coral reefs, and fireflies
We will wonder why we didn't do more
As Mother Earth dies.

Lighthouse

These vast open spaces; burned down to bare
bones.
Subliminal and bright and emotive and solemn.
Here we met, in this sensational place.
A chasmic love.
Deeper than romance, stronger than blood.
We travel steadily, bound together by the beating
of uncertainty.
Even in the slowest moments, in the absolute
stillness, boundless radiance finds us.
This is what I've been craving.
To be both exhausted and fulfilled.
To cherish these moments of adoration,
sublimation, and depth.
I am finally at peace.
Time after time, we are drawn to each other.
We are two souls intertwined on a perpetual
journey,
I am the river, and you are the sea,
At times we are chaos, others serene.
In the darkness, you light up hope and
I beacon you home.
No matter the distance, the ebb of the tides
brings us together.

A Sisyphean Hell of moving mountains to
belong
Only to realize that together is home.
I don't know what I would do without you,
For you are my twin star, my soulmate, my
lighthouse in a stormy sea.

Mud Puddles and Dandelions

When I think of my childhood, I think of toys and games, of laughing and crying, of scrapes and scabs and the adventures that caused them; but most of all, I think of mud puddles and dandelions. I was always an outdoorsy kind of girl. I loved animals and I loved nature. It wasn't like I was purely a tomboy. I mean, sure it was fun getting dirty and playing pirates or cops and robbers, but I liked dress up and house as well. I loved to dress up in beautiful dresses and then go play in the dirt or catch frogs from the pond. My mom realized quickly to buy my clothes second hand because they were going to be ruined the first day that I wore them.

I never thought that I would miss mud so much. Or hate those yellow flowers with such a passion. But things change when you get older; the feeling of mud squishing between your toes becomes disgusting. You worry about the microscopic parasites and disease that could be in the stagnant sludge. And what you once thought were pretty flowers turn into monstrous weeds that consume and leech nutrients from the garden. It is nearly every day I wish Peter Pan would come and whisk me away to Neverland.

It doesn't have to be this way; I could try splashing in the mud, but just think of how dirty my shoes would be afterwards. And I pay for my own shoes these days. I wish I could rub a dandelion on the top of my hand to see if I 'liked butter'. But I've developed an allergy to them, and I would break into hives. Then pay for the doctor visit or a medicated cream.

Adulthood really just seems to be spending money on things that you need: gas, food, electricity, water; money, money, MONEY. I never get to buy things for myself anymore. If I want it, it's usually not needed, so I wait. So far, I'm not seeing the appeal of being an adult. Sure, being on my own is fun. For the most part, I can do what I want, when I want. I can eat ice cream for breakfast and stay up all night. But those decisions have unfortunate consequences in and of themselves. When I'm sick, I have no mommy to rub my back and take care of me. I don't get to stop to play in the rain because I have to shuffle to work or some other menial appointment. Instead of being excited to see bunnies in the garden, I shoo them away because I can't have them eating the vegetables.

I don't have children of my own, and I still want to wait awhile. But I look forward to sharing the magic of the world with them. I can watch them run through the sprinkler and roll down clover-covered hills. They will know Santa Claus and the Tooth Fairy on a personal level; writing letters of gratitude and hope to their heroes. They'll wish on shooting stars and toss pennies into fountains. They'll dance in the rain and collapse into puddles. And collect dandelions, yellow in the spring, and flocculent white wisps in the fall. They'll blow the seeds into dispersion and not care that they are spreading weeds, because dandelions will be their favorite flower.

How do we bring the magic of our youth into adulthood? How do we carry the purity and innocence of being carefree into a world where it seems mandatory to be riddled with anxiety and frustration? I suppose we start with simple things: mud puddles and dandelions. We dance in the rain, stomp in the puddles; we bring our dreams and hopes to light and allow ourselves a fleeting moment of silliness to wish on the scattering of a weed. After all, what are weeds but merely wildflowers with the longing to thrive?